FINNA

poems

Nate Marshall

ONE WORLD
NEW YORK

A One World Trade Paperback Original

Copyright © 2020 by Nathaniel A. Marshall

All rights reserved.

Published in the United States by One World, an imprint of Random House, a division of Penguin Random House LLC, New York.

ONE WORLD and Design is a registered trademark of Penguin Random House LLC.

Some of the poems in this work were published in the Academy of American Poets Poem-a-Day, *The Adroit Journal, BOATT Journal, Chicago, Columbia Poetry Review, The Fight & The Fiddle, Kenyon Review Online, The Offing, Poetry, The Shallow Ends, Split Lip Magazine,* and *The Rumpus,* and in THE END OF CHIRAQ (Evanston, IL: Northwestern University Press, 2018).

LIBRARY OF CONGRESS CATALOGING-IN-PUBLICATION DATA
Names: Marshall, Nate (Poet) author.
Title: Finna : poems / by Nate Marshall.
Description: First Edition. | New York : One World, [2020]
Identifiers: LCCN 2020006231 (print) | LCCN 2020006232 (ebook) | ISBN 9780593132456 (trade paperback) | ISBN 9780593132463 (ebook)
Subjects: LCGFT: Poetry.
Classification: LCC PS3613.A77555 F56 2020 (print) | LCC PS3613.A77555 (ebook) | DDC 811/.6—dc23
LC record available at https://lccn.loc.gov/2020006231
LC ebook record available at https://lccn.loc.gov/2020006232

Printed in the United States of America on acid-free paper

randomhousebooks.com
oneworldlit.com

9 8 7 6 5 4 3 2 1

FIRST EDITION

Book design by Simon M. Sullivan

For my people, the ones I love &
especially the ones I struggle to love

this dark diction has become america's addiction.

—MALIK YUSEF

among the Blacks is misery enough, God knows, but no poetry.

—some white boy

Contents

The Other Nate Marshall

What's My Favorite Word?

Native Informant

FINNA

FINNA

landless acknowledgment

before we get started we would like to acknowledge that we live on some unceded bones. sometimes me & mine imagine ancestral homes. all i got so far is Montgomery, Alabama. maybe a boat. maybe a plot of land somewhere so far from the south sides i've claimed that i would get lost on the way. i admit sometimes my homies talk about their families immigrating & i get jealous. we lost the land we were custodians over before i was a twinkle in the eye of a twinkle in the eye of a twinkle in the eye. closest i got to a homeland is my mama's caucasian pitch on the phone calling the police. closest i got to a homeland is not never calling the police. closest i got to a homeland is my daddy's laugh in a spades game. closest i got to a homeland is my lover's tongue talking or otherwise. closest i got to a homeland is the funk under a DJ's needle & my hand full of a dance partner. not to be dark but i am. not to be dark but the planet is on fire. not to be dark but our bones are in that water too. maybe that's my capital? once the polar capitals melt & there's a whole lot less land for folks to buy & sell & steal maybe everybody will feel a little more dark. will feel a little more homelandless like we do. why you think i call my compatriots homies? maybe ain't no home except for how your beloveds cuss or pray or pronounce.

The Other Nate Marshall

keep my name out your mouth cuz you can't handle the fleek.

—JAMILA WOODS

**Nate Marshall is a white supremacist from Colorado
or Nate Marshall is a poet from the South Side of
Chicago or i love you Nate Marshall**

when i first made
my name Nate
i was a boy
at summer camp
looking for cool
in the muggy shadow
& so when the white boys
snipped Nathaniel
to just a touch of the tongue
to the mouth roof
it seemed to me
a religious moment,
a new confirmation as okay.

this was 2000 &
you must have been
Nate Marshall
for decades by then.

i find you, years later,
buried in a google search
& follow you silently
for the next year
like a high school crush.

i tell my students about you
the day when we wonder what if
privilege hadn't put us in
a college classroom.

i tell my ex about you in bed
& it's convenient that there's this other
Nate Marshall to be the liar
lying there this time.

i see your failed campaign & watch how your ties
to white supremacists spelled your demise.
my Black history month paper on the Black Panthers
in 3rd grade wouldn't color me radical enough & i am ashamed
i've never been pushed out of a spotlight for loving
my people too much. your day job is roofing & i just watch HGTV
in hotels. you are the truer amongst us Nate. you, peddler of
    propaganda
& seller of shingles.

can you show me to love how you love?

every time i've said *what's good nigga*
it's possible we've matched
our mouths, symmetrical
around the two g's in the middle.

i won't lie to you Nate Marshall
or to myself Nate Marshall
i too have hated a nigga & lived
to tweet the tale.
i too have sat suspicious in my basement
wondering who was coming for my country.

i too have googled myself & found a myself
i despise.

once, you left Twitter
after i told my people to tell you
that they loved you & your book
& your commitment to Black people
& i feel you Nate Marshall.
i've left places & loves
when they told me they loved
a Nate Marshall
i didn't recognize.

another Nate Marshall origin story

so, for the purposes of this story let's say
turn of the 20th century my great
grandfather Marshall disappeared
so thoroughly nobody know what he looks like.

so let's say he's super high yellow
so much so maybe he's swarthy
if he stays out of sun & so
in this story he drops my grandpops
& then pulls out of Mississippi to step west
& stretch his legs as a white man.

so let's say he has a whole white
family with a little boy.
& let's say he overcorrects
cuz he knows the color
the boy carries without knowing
so he tells the little boy
we don't associate with those people
& that little boy has a whole lineage
who don't talk to those people.

so, maybe the name Marshall is just a passing
story we'll never uncover. maybe he secret
Black like a Hollywood actor. but maybe
he knows & wants his name back
     & his body too.

my daddy's daddy's daddy or the etymology of Marshall

or a blank space
>   or a space filled
>   or a filled job
>   or a job vacant
or a vacant lot
>   or a lot of questions
>   or a question posed
or a 'posed to & ain't
>   or a ain't known
>   or a known forgotten
>   or a forgotten name
>   or a name left
>   or a left us.

another Nate Marshall origin story

again the white me
on the internet appears
& this time he wants
what is his.

our name
is a country
he claims
for himself.

you need to quit
using my name.
it is not your name. you are
fake! i am Nate Marshall. you are
filth!

Nate Marshall calls Nate Marshall
all this.

every Nate Marshall i know
has an unruly name
                    a word he can't trace back.

one Nate Marshall deletes
himself.

every Nate Marshall i know
is mistaken.

how to pronounce Nathaniel

the southern folk say the a out long ways
pull it apart so the syllables hang loose
as laundry on the clothesline.

the schools i went to,
top ranked & unimaginative,
make it obvious, unimpressive, a stub of an uh sound
compact & efficiently packaged.

my mama says it how she always has
but i can never remember her intonation.
this little blip,   where I   forget my   self.

beloved, how you say it though,
that's the way it's said.
i know when you say me
like i'm an incantation
i know i ain't no lie.

another Nate Marshall origin story

when the obscure meaning
of the name
is no longer an unreachable itch

the mouth will fall away,
both plump lips will dry
& drop from the stupid face.

imagine this, a man
made donut, chest open,
hollow, everything poured
out, available, nowhere
to drum a warning, no place to
keep out.

perhaps our rage
at the other is just the way
we fill what we don't know
about ourselves.

nigger joke

so this nigger walks into a bar in this gentrifying neighborhood &
orders fried chicken & the nigger gets a craft beer cuz the nigger
went to graduate school & the nigger is waiting for his fried chicken
& this white man walks up & sits down in front of a half drank tall-
boy & calls the nigger's phone a big ass phone & the nigger laughs
because the phone is big & bought for with his graduate school
money & the nigger keeps his eyes up at the football game & the
white man extends his hand & the nigger takes it with kool-aid
strained cheeks because the nigger thinks about this week & all the
wrong that white people have done & maybe this is a start of a dif-
ferent story & maybe the white man will tell him something honest
over the liquor & buy him drinks & so the white man asks the nigger
if he knows the neighborhood but the nigger is new around here so
the white man says *welcome* & assures the nigger *this is a good bar* the
white man talks about how he's here most nights & has never seen a
fight & he talks about how whites & niggers & latinos drink in peace
& talks about the last 10 years & the buildings he bought a decade
ago that are multiplying his pockets & the white man talks about his
catholic school past & the white man talks about making a corridor
from downtown to the suburbs & he's waiting for the other shoe to
drop always & cop more buildings & get more rents & he asks the
nigger where he's from & the nigger says south side & the white man
tells the nigger what south side is & the white man talks about "cop
blocks" & assures the nigger all of south side isn't a wasteland be-
cause there's "cop blocks" over there too & the nigger tries to shift
the conversation to the south side white neighborhoods because the
nigger went to elementary school in one & the white man talks
about those cousins he has there & how they are on an island & how
the south side is so bad but not where the white folks live & the nig-

ger tries the college town he lived in & the white man's dad went to school there & the white man got in but white man's dad wouldn't pay for that school even on his judge salary so the white man went military academy instead & the white man got cop brothers & other family & the white man talks about his second house in the state of the college town & how up there he's a catholic & the not catholic white men look at him different when they find out & then the white man says *i never been oppressed except one time* & he says *in Virginia everybody's a nigger* & the nigger says nothing the nigger eats his chicken which got there a while ago & listens to the nigger joke & the nigger joke says nothing & looks at the football game & the white man says *pardon me if saying the nigger word offends you* but the nigger joke just nods & the nigger joke waits for the white man to finish his story & the nigger joke eats the chicken with a singular focus & hopes the bone plunges into his throat & the nigger joke isn't hungry & can't stop eating as fast as possible & the nigger joke hopes the white man stops talking about the protestors who are probably college students who should probably protest college tuition & not cops doing their jobs but the nigger joke isn't listening the nigger joke is repeating the prayer his mama taught him & the prayer starts with the good elementary school & then the good high school & then the excellent college & then the incredible graduate school & how it was all merit scholarship & also the high test scores including the awards & honors of course the publications & acclaim & the nigger joke finishes his prayer & the nigger joke sees somebody's prayer answered when the nigger joke pays the waitress & tells the white man have a good night & cries the walk home.

nah nah this one though is for all my niggas

       starting with my Black niggas
& assorted non-white niggas
& even some white niggas!
even the other Nate Marshall . . .
actually especially him.

what up to all the Nate Marshalls!
there's a hockey player
& a comedian
& 1 on acoustic guitar
&

1 time a dude i knew hit me up relieved & shaken
when his timeline told him Nate Marshall had been murdered
but it was a different me somewhere on the North Side.

definitely peace to that Nate Marshall
& to his people who would have been relieved
had i been the news article instead of their sweet, beautiful boy.

love to y'all & to all the me's not here to still be stupid.
all the me's not around to make mistakes & make amends.
all the me's who are fertilizer & not growing theyselves no more.

family, this is my name
& a myth that i don't own alone. i never even meant
to have this name this just a happy accident of birth,
an unhappy coincidence of intersecting histories,
an abbreviation that became law.

look niggas, Nathaniel became Nate & is both. true story.
did y'all niggas know i meet siblings every day
who change they name to touch they truths? i know
that. & i know there's finna be at least 1 nigga who read
this poem out loud when they know they ain't got no good
business with my name in they mouth. i know there's finna be
at least 1 nigga who email me to ask why i gotta use
such an ugly word to call myself & my people
& i'm just gonna respond & say which word? i been had a few
names the world gave me & then won't call me. i been had a name
soft & pliant as a tonal language. i been had a name
that was offensive or a love song depending
on who held it in they mouth.

What's My Favorite Word?

we should always be guarding against every evil
word . . .

—JUPITER HAMMON

everything i've called women

if i said baby you might think love but nah.
that's only maybe what i mean, perhaps i'll say ma

& your mind says Cam'ron, women creeping up
but i'm a changed man, & that's not game ma.

it's high school & THOT isn't out yet
we're classic Chicago & bustdowns bloom in our mouths. my Ma

spits Too $hort & the line i catch the first time
is *b*tch b*tch b*tch make me rich* but Ma

puts me on punishment when i whisper Ludacris
& tells me sex shouldn't hurt. i say nothing & Ma

lets it go until a few years later when i get becky
or brain or top or dome by a white girl & Ma

tells me everything i've risked for this escapade.
i can't fix my mouth to say   *but Ma*

what i got i didn't ask for. shorty just kinda went
& i was supposed to moan street things like *hey ma*

you sexy as hell. & after that i say it all
& give women a rash of nicknames there's ma

(who calls me pa) & Hollywood & princess & pop star
& doctor & lady & kneesocks & *yo ma*

i missed your name i just put where we met in my phone
don't be mad i remember our whole convo ma

& bae & baby & honey & shorty & poison & tenderoni
& when i'm lonely *hey stranger. how you been ma?*

& sometimes i've called & gotten dial tone songs
or been told Nate do you remember my name? or is that why you
   say ma?

my mom's favorite rapper was Too $hort

before i could talk
i could stalk Oakland streets
in my mind. i'm a cussword

pitched at the tip of a tongue
sung like an omen. women
were the first i saw hum this

lullaby. my mama told me
about the white house & selling
cocaine, nancy reagan's business

prowess. my big sister helped me count
cold cash money—slap
snaps at suckers like a pimp.

you motherfuckers thought
i was gon' change my style?
all the while i'm here holding

what i learned. by the time i was 5
i knew *man you still alive?*
by heart, the hardest lyric

in our whole song. i'm the age
to be that plot twist now. how
can i unlearn some of the curses

that were the first
spells i saw conjured?
i wrote this rhyme

for you.
you might not
like my rap

& you'd be right.
you might be
right

& not be
true.
you might be

true
& not be
you.

we all have our pleasures
we're guilty about
not feeling guilty about.

we all look for the radical
reframing that lets
our ass shake.

we all gaze in the mirror, mouth
our favorite word without speech.
even without volume we hear it,

we all watch
ourselves,
ask:

if not these perjured women,
who will *make me*
rich.

with no invitation

a boy is taken.
but here's a question:
a boy says yes under what circumstance?

trick question. a boy
doesn't say anything
unless he's asked.

trick answer. she didn't
know what to say.

trick answer. he's a shade of
hesitant but maybe
he's game.

bald fade

Richard could slice a nigga from fro to caesar in 17 flat. he, dream genius of diminishing Black curl. he used to pick me up Saturday mornings, stop & cop me McDonald's hot cakes. he sat me in the back of the shop while opening. let me eat & then readied me for the slice. the bald fade. the 90s cut up front, neat. the back graphics. the rounded fro. the cornrow lining. the Michael Jordan/Daddy deluxe. my head a democratic laboratory for nap possibility. my head lived in Richard's hands—Richard was our family friend. haircut-on-credit close. hand-me-candy-store-money close. leave-me-the-*Curtis*-comic-strips close. first-school-dance-get-me-right close. down-the-street close. try-to-fuck-my-sister close. never-went-to-prison close. check-his-sex-offender-registry-listing close. map-the-route-to-his-house close. consider-repaying-his-cut close. saw him at the gas station last summer. walked right past my pump, close. he, who made my wave pattern, didn't recognize me at the pump after hair loss & decades-plus of thickening into man. he would only know me from the way my dome pinches slightly up front, a mark he made when he gave my first fade.

only boy

when i was 6 my grandmother gave me
a single dollar for pushing a girl
to the concrete during double dutch.
the girl, nameless now in my head,
was a head taller & 3 years older
& believed my face looked best streaked red
by the clotheswire.

                    when Kay-Kay baby sat us as toddlers
                    she would sling my tough hair
                    into small puffs with her barrette balls.
                    mama asked her why.

in 7th grade i dry humped high school girls
to juke mixes in basements as unfinished as i.
my reason for being at those parties was
to chaperone a sister 10 months my senior.

i never knew the business end of a curfew,
took the city by train anywhere i could imagine.
mama told me be home by the time
                i was alive.

                    still young & praying over a rare family dinner.
                    my voice cracks through the uncertain absolution
                    we all hold hands, mine no bigger than theirs.

i did not talk much. i say little now
that i mean with my whole self in public.
i am whipped with jump rope
or i am pushing.

as a baby i didn't start talking until late.
my sister suggested i go to a special doctor
to inspect my head
to see where the language had gone.

all my sisters huddle into the car
to go together. girls' night. i watch them leave.
i hold a book in front of my face.

my granddaddy sees the streets

       & knows all the boys
are punks. he doesn't
believe in thugs
or boogeymen. what he sees is
little men who never got a proper
whipping. all these little men
with no hands, no mind for stick & move. guns
for these new boys are no metaphor.

my granddaddy is from the fair one.

my granddaddy saw *Rocky* & started training to box
in his 40s. roadwork down the dim streets,
hands up & swinging at any boy bad enough
to take the discipline. half a lifetime before that he got beat
by his old man for being bad & he became a bad
man with hands heavy as a sad sad story.

now his memory stumbles like taking a solid hit
& in the end all he can promise
his people in the streets
is an ass whooping.

epicene

a justification of slavery said
Blacks were the lady
of the races. in this logic
the bondage is an overcoat
over the puddle.

the whitefolk said, Black, as in
not men. Black, as in not woman. Black,
as in this brutality is just benevolence.

if this the case
call me sis. if this
the case then here
is me, not a man
but a query. if this
the case then fuck
whatever freedom
given by this hand.
if this the case *bitch*
ass nigga is redundant.

i don't mean slave logic
holds but i mean
all our traps are inventions
of the same lazy tongue.

what i know is:
i'm Black sure

& i'm as much man
as my pops & his.

what i know is:
most of who held me
down has been Black
women.

what i know is:
i want to be as much
man as mama & grandmama
who brought home fatback & headed households.

what i know is:
sometimes all of my sisters have a girls'
night & i don't have any brothers
& sometimes it's okay
& other times i want my invitation.

darla: i don't know when - April 7, 2016

after francine j. harris

its not that i didn't like you
its more that you were never
much of anything to me except always
around. here you are riding my granddaddy's
back outside of our house when y'all showed
up drunk again & us kids were the only ones there.
you again at thanksgiving saying something
stupid that we all ignore & then saying it
again.

its not that i didn't like you
its more that you were never
very smart. the type of woman
to have to think about the question
when asked her own name. the kind
of woman to take up with a married
man & never seem to feel
anything on the subject.

its not that i didn't like you
its more my mama didn't.
couldn't fucking stand you.
its not her fault but she couldn't
hate her daddy for his sins & so
you gotta hold this one down on his behalf.

its not that i didn't like you
its more i barely knew your name

growing up. you were just
hussy or *tramp* or *slut* or
grandma looking teary eyed
at the deflated speed bag in the basement.

its not that i didn't like you
its more i never expected you to die
which is stupid when i saw you never
really lived your own life.
you just granddaddy's shadow,
same stumble & bad brain,
same sweet pride over this selfish
boy named Armstead.

its not that i didn't like you
its more i just never like
thought about you for real.

its not that i didn't like you
its more i didn't know you had kids
or siblings. i didn't know
you were like a real person.

forgive me, this selfish boy named Armstead
who stopped in his tracks when he saw your mama
collect the extra obituaries saying *i need these*
i need to tell anybody who come by
about my baby. my sweet sweet child.

the homies ask if i'm tryna smash

our language for sex:

stain   *smash*

                    this is where we live
                    a land of impact & soiling,
                    a gaggle of boys boasting
                    over hurt. our tongues
                    wagging, stupid flags
                    of a dumb dominion. our love
                    for each other measured
bang   in what we lord over. we poor   *beat*
                    timekeepers, consider our preposition here:
                    bros before _____.
                    we anti-historians. we unmakers of ourselves.
                    we failures of science & courage.
                    we ugly. we ugly. we ugly.
                    we a bankrupt vernacular,
                    a slang as prophecy,
                    a linguistic imperative towards
                    pain.

hit   *pound*

step

learn this or get out my house
is how mama started my dance lesson
when i was a boy.

                                       & mama was off
          & suddenly she was high school sized
          & spinning a hole into our old carpet.

the basic is letting the bottom of each heel tap
& snap back to the beat.

                    you only gotta find one simple step
                    & you can always come home
                    to that after anything fancy
                    you might try.

first you gotta follow
& then lead
& once you & your partner are real
enough there really ain't no lead.

                    in Chicago we call it steppin'
                    but perhaps every Black
                    neighborhood has some version
                    they call swing or bop or hand dance or hustle.

i mean to dance, to take my partner's
hands & spin in such a way our bodies blend
into a single downbeat.

your auntie don't understand why your great uncle such a no count negro & in general why men resolve to be no count dogs for no good reason

       & its not her job to know
why men be wrong
as often as days got y's at they back
but if i didn't tell you i'd be a negligent uncle
so sit down & poke your chest back
in before i make you concave. here it is:
sick boy. we all sick. you drink bad
water you gon' have bad blood that's just good
sense. you ever seen a pit bull with a heavy head
& a body sliding into nothing?
well a dog starving like that might not eat.
he was proli beat, maybe lame in a leg or missin'
an ear. that dog proli got half his teeth & none
of his mean gone. he proli attack you when you try
to help. he proli sink his one good tooth
right in your leg even if it kills him.
that dog is a danger but its like this.
that dog didn't train himself.
that dog learned early a kill
is the way to a meal.

an uncle's fable for consent

i'm trying to find language to talk about these things.
—AJA MONET

check it out nephew
what it be like is this:
you ever touch the open palm
of a cold iron? best shit
you could put on the soft
side of your face, like sweet
jesus kissing you on the cheek.
but you gotta check anything
you aim to touch beforehand
otherwise you might end up
messed up. & the messed up
thing about the burn is you don't
feel it at first. the body shock
itself into apathy but after that
it sting & smooth & bubble &
break open & grow back nasty enough
to ugly up a baby face motherfucker.
that's a kind of scar you keep
& the thing about it is even after you don't
feel it everybody see it & you do
once your simple ass look in a mirror.

memoir of a wronger

nah boo. you just fuckin wit the wrong niggas.
— a wronger nigga

the truth is
ima pimp
or a pusher.
ima drug
who needs
to be dragged
i'm dressed
to the 9s
performing
for whoever.

i'm out here
on this bridge
called i'm buck
wild give a fuck
less what i hurt
with my hurt.
i'm a smirk
after the explosion.

the truth is
relative
like your cousin
who borrowed
that money &

been in the wind
since.

the truth is
relative
like your uncle
who ain't allowed
in granny house
after those
troubles,
you know.

look me in my eyes girl:
i [redacted] you.
you can [redacted] me.
give me your [redacted].
i'll be your [redacted].

**poem in which I consider my artistic
& romantic life via *Purple Rain***

maybe it was a stupid subconscious allusion
when i insisted to my boy Shaun
our rap group be called the revolution.

we didn't understand political upheaval. we just listened
to Talib & Mos & thought the word ripe
in our 13-year-old mouths. now, decades later, i suspect
it was more our mothers' happy whole body
shudders when the radio DJ threw it
back to "1999" that gave us the idea
for the name.

something about moving a woman
in such a complete way seemed
a good idea & dangerous
enough to name a rap group.
two little dudes who couldn't play
any instrument past middle school
trying to call ourselves the name
of the symbol's backup band.
we were delusional.

in my family's basement's VHS collection
between some old porn, Michael Jackson's
Moonwalker, & *VeggieTales Bible Stories*
sat *Purple Rain.* damn, those scenes played
like a Lord's prayer.

in the days my dad didn't call
for weeks & then called to talk about
a baseball game neither of us gave a fuck about
what i wouldn't have given for a swift kick
& cuss to run away from.

in my mom's 3 job era i wished
for someone home enough for me
to need a club to escape to.

in the summer i fell
for my own Nikki & all the cool the raps gave me went away.

in the summer i fell
for my own Nikki & renamed myself something unpronounceable.

in the summer i fell
for my own Nikki but i rode away from her
at the lake & never circled back.

telling stories

a few times each year
i am convinced of the end
of singleness, the beginning
of a singularity, i become convinced
of the infinite curve of love.

my grandma, like all Black grandmothers
perhaps, told me do not *tell stories*
by which she meant do not *lie* except we couldn't say lie
which was a curse word in her house.

my grandma, like all Black grandmothers
perhaps, told me stories about where we were
from, & who we were from, & the unbroken string
of happy accidents & hapless miracles that made us possible.

my grandma used to say *worse thing in the world a liar or a thief*
& i know i have been both these most deplored before.

my grandma used to say *i love you.*

my grandma gone.
my convictions gone too.
does that mean an end
to the long curve of her love
or mine?

does that mean *i love you*
is always bound to end up
a story? If so what kind?
the worst thing or
one of the small impossibilities
that put us here.

the best story is about home because that's the story part

so tell me what you call me when i'm not around.
—NONAME

often i be out &
about the words
moving quotes to the folks
like a fix.

don't understand?
feel me this way:
the other day i was walking
through the old hood to see
me in the cheap duplexes
& all the wrong houses were
vacant &
some of our board ups
were blooming with new boys.

the last time i went to the church of my birth
all the old folks looked the same kind
of hard starched sharp they always been
& i been gone so long nobody
asked where i been.

look, every time i show up
at the function
it's a surprise
party to my homies.

all i call my people
is what i say in they absence.

peep the props i cop from how hard
i represent the spots i hardly hit
but hail from.

feel me: she told me i didn't
give her my best hours & i told her
here's more & started pulling clocks
out my pockets & she said its time
to go 'head on.

took a L fam

no, not the train that steak knifes
through the city.

no, not brown paper twisted & honey sealed
for a slow burn.

no, not another name for God——
though perhaps prayer is in order

just another leaving
another heart handed back——
politely or not.

just another
or nah
for the list.

just another night alternating
the side of the mattress
i sleep on
to keep it even.

ode to vacation

O vacation you are a word i know
the meaning of but don't know.

when i was young
there was the lone family trip
to a water park in Wisconsin.

in college there was the week we had
in South Carolina with my best friend's family.
we went on plantation tours to see
the beautiful gardens & all i could see
was blood & flowers. i still wonder who keeps ground
on those plots now, though i bet i can guess.

vacation, we met again in Guatemala
& i asked not to but we are here
with an ex-love because the flights were paid
& the trip planned. on the plane home she got an upgrade
to first class & had me sit next to her since the seat was empty
though i was still coach. 45 minutes into the flight
they checked my ticket &
i got moved back
where i belonged.

vacation, i don't get you or rather
i don't give you the time & i don't take
the time off. it's my lineage dear vacation.
i'm from 2 jobs at minimum
& retiring only to turn the house into

a home business. the story goes
that more than one of my relations
used to visit dope houses in their work
uniforms & maybe the high is also an occupation.

vacation, i have tax forms & under the table work
falling out of my head like hair.
i haven't seen a week of mine end since
i was at least 18.

vacation, you a lie & i don't lie
down for much of anything these days.

sweet breath

lover, all that slang we swapped
between our regions won't do
much for us now. how could it?
there's no word for us
except our names & what is
a secret if i say it
in front of company?

remember us, a late night
when everybody else is asleep or pretending
& we are awake & not watching
nothing but each other. we call each other *my nigga.*
this pet name we exchange will make the voyeur
think animal or abomination
& i have no reason to correct
when what we on this eve could be either
or both.

forget the good schools we attended, the degrees.
all the big words & eloquent expletives
we bandy about for fun are missing tonight.
i can't say   anything
but heavy breath   our new language
for yes
with your writing hand wrapped around my windpipe.

the valley of its making

poetry makes nothing happen
—W. H. AUDEN

the people in the streets
are plucked up like
radishes from dark earth,
heads beat the purplish red
of ripeness. the women lead
the stupid & brutish to a
future they don't deserve.
the organized are still
unbearably human, they
still fuck & hurt & harm
& are not actually sorry.
the people still fight
each other too much &
the system not enough
& too often it is not a fight
but a bullet. too many men
want to be in the front
& don't want to march
anywhere in particular.
some of us have degrees
& noses to look down.
so many want a version
of old days that never
existed. many are still unwilling
to grow a vocabulary for personhood,
even from the words already in them.

so many will deny *they* to a sibling
simply because. our people are
messy & messed up & a mess.
nothing about our people is romantic
& it shouldn't be. our people deserve
poetry without meter. we deserve our
own jagged rhythm & our own uneven
walk towards sun. you make happening happen.
we happen to love. this is our greatest
action.

Harold's Chicken Shack #2

ask any mug on the South Side
& they'll say their own particular
alchemy for appetite.
we each have an intersection
we'll point you to on
the day of the week
when the grease
is the right kind of dirty.

> *boy don't say nothing if you ain't been to 103rd & Halsted*
> *on a Wednesday . . .*

> *me myself i'm more 64th & Cottage any Thursday before 4 . . .*

> *better hit 87th off the Ryan before them other folk get wind &*
> *take that too.*

truth is
there are more Chicken Shacks
than anybody care to count
& the number is always growing or shrinking
depending on the day.

truth is
some of them ain't all that.

truth is
some of them have off days
or decades.

truth is
there is more than 1 with sauce
sweet enough
to sponge up with white bread.

what she taught me
when she picked me up
& poured into me
is ain't nobody got a monopoly
on your hope or your good feeling
or your proper crunch
or your sweet sweet spice.

habitual

i be but i don't is. i been & i
am one who be on my own biz. i love
not a b____. but see know i been loved. i'm
one who been that & then not deserved much

cuz i been on my own dirt. i don't know
love. i been a lie but don't be a lie
i be fly sometimes but don't be a fly
sometimes i be addict like but not high

like an addict's like. just scratching low stones
like an addict might. stop? not an option.
i be getting mine. been getting over.
been over this but be caught in a cycle.

but you be what you be & it be good.
& i be moved & making new habits.

Native Informant

i'm deprogramming y'all wit' uncut slang shit.
—Black Thought

when i say Chicago

capital city of the flyover.
crown jewel of the jailhouse.
a town in love with its own blood,
a blood browned on its own history & funk.
hometown of the riot & the riot gear,
the gang & the loitering law.
misfit blocks of dark-skinned cousins &
thick knuckled slavic uncles
who call each other their worst names.

what this country know 'bout a rustbelt
dipped in salt & vinegar & sold as
marked up & rustic?

my city is the city.
not your close enough suburb not
subject to the suppression of tape
& the tapping of phones.
how can you say anything about our blocks
& schools & children that you refuse to see.
don't tell us what is wrong
with all of our cousins you've never known.
you do not govern what you do not love.

when i say Chicago
i mean that first Haitian cat who could pronounce it right.

when i say Chicago
i mean the stopped & frisked.
i mean the euphemism of frisk.
i mean the beat down & tight cuff.
i mean the drop-off in Bridgeport
or Mount Greenwood.
i mean the lessons
taught to an uppity one.

when i say Chicago
i mean the lake
(& i mean all of it).
i mean the candy lady at Rainbow
& the paleta man at Calumet
& the kids careening across the green at Montrose
& the jogger in midwinter daring a death for fitness

when i say Chicago
i mean Cabrini & Stateway & Ickes & Ida,
the city i'll tell my kids about in the past tense.
i mean the rents that sometimes
make me mean Georgia or Indiana or Dolton.

when i say Chicago i mean
the restaurants with no chairs
just a window, a bulletproof sneeze guard.
i mean a Michelin star for all the ethnics slanging
their seasoned meats & language.

when i say Chicago i mean my mama's
house that was my grandma's house.

i mean the neighborhood
that was our neighborhood
because we said
we'll make a home here
& we'll stay.

another Nate Marshall origin story

so Nate Marshall moves to Colorado
years after Nate Marshall moved to Colorado
that's what always happens.

moving is, perhaps, the single largest commonality amongst
   everything living.

& don't get me wrong
i'm not saying i'm like him
i'm just saying i'm not not.

i'm just saying a person is a person
cuz people. even the ones we'd rather not.

even the Nate Marshalls who ain't me
are me & i because of them. & even the Nate Marshalls
who seem most fixed in their place
might move
if they're alive.

scruples

        is the word i tell anyone who asks
for my favorite. what sounded
to me like a doctor's instrument was just a
name for the hesitation respectability births.

O, small keeper of my failure
at the 4th grade spelling bee.
i loved the way my mouth cupped your vowels
like a spoonful of newly cooled soup. you
were my convenient bae or beau or note
with a multiple-choice admission of admiration
but you are not my most honest longing.

when i'm alone in my room
or at my family's cookout
or at the basketball courts
i spill finna from my mouth
like 2 cheeks full of pop
punctured with a laugh. everywhere
my finna exists it's a warning or heckle or plea bargain
telling myself, or my mama, or this motherfucker that's
been jawing all game everything i'm about to turn into;
all the hesitation i shook loose.

slave grammar

Lol Chicago slang be dumb as hell
Whole time & don't nobody be knowing
how to explain what it mean
we all just got a understanding

—@_GOMP on Twitter 27 Jul 2014

this not proper,
this people.
this a failing school
meet a magnet program.
trick question,
they kin.
this no question,
this answer—
ancestral.
this be habitual.
this the dirty words
lined up in they baddest fits.
this that this that
bad meaning _____
you know what i mean.
you know what i'm saying
whole time i'm bending the language
like a bow every arrow is spinning itself
a new sharp tip. whole time
i'm writing this down its obsoleting
itself. whole time we talking we ain't got
no dictionary we guessing the spelling
we deciphering the phrases through

our slurs we slurring like we ain't sure until
we murmur a sure vow. whole time
we blur the whole thing
we make shambles of their standards
we stand on them
& fashion an abolition
in diction.

WITH THANKS TO SEAN DESVIGNES

only I for whitefolk using Black language

you a guest.
welcome. now clean
your feet & say hi
to my mama. if she say
she ain't hear you
say hi until she does,
this her house.

when my nephew walk in
& ask you who is you, you answer.
when my uncle, drunk, drips
who is you, you answer.
when my baby cousin's first sentence
is a query concerning you, you answer.
when my granddaddy ask who is you
& then who is you again
a few times, you answer each time with
a soft smile & a tip of your hat.

this ain't your house.
even though you welcome
& you can & should eat & get full
& two-step to the radio
& talk smack at the card table
& stay as long as you like
like you fam.

but fam, understand, if you treat the fam
like strangers, then you a stranger, fam.

Oo Wop De Bam

by the time you get this transmission
we'll already be off this planet
or on the bus heading downtown
scratch bombing our last will & testament
into some commuter's view. here's the thing:

everything you don't know is intentional.
either by you or by us. don't act like you mad
you can't hear the words we radio edited out.
you remember that scene in *White Men Can't Jump*
when the question of listening & hearing is raised.

you knew then that there could be nothing between us
except rhythmic static. you know our whole dialect
is a rawhide stretched into a handclap, a record scratch,
a jive so unintelligible it must be genius.
you seen us leaning against the whole world with one foot up,
cocked back like a prayer.

you seen us in your corporate offices. creeping in Black
as something Black & live. we know your slang too.
better than you. we invented that & gave it to you
for whatever winter equinox holiday you prefer.
we know African american is how you say nigger in a boardroom.

we're hip to your myriad of words for desertion or starvation or
   genocide.
even our conversation filler is a conjuring. the dark cousin
of your *whatchamacallit* & *thingamajig*.
our whole steez a code you can't break, can't even dent,
can't fade in the least & we see you finna try.

a poem for Justin

because you asked for one
when i told you to stop jumping on me
that night as i was writing.

because your favorite Jay-Z song
is "December 4th"—for his mother's voice
& Jay's story about his life.

because i told you the first song you heard
in your young life was "I Used to Love H.E.R."
in the hospital room with my big headphones
over your soft head.

because you asked me your first word
& i said i didn't know
& i could have told you a good lie
& made that a small poem we shared.

because when you spend the night
you take my clothes
& drape them over yourself like a prayer shawl.

because you clown me
to my friends &
impersonate me in a way
that says *i see you uncle*.

because you ask me if i love all books
since i have so many & i say
only the ones that tell us who we are.

because i ask you
what i should write about
& you say
write about us.

On _____

the highest promise we could offer
was one to a land or man or idea
greater than we. someone would exclaim
on folk i made that shot or *on*
chief i got her number or *on*
boss i didn't see anything that night.
when we put covenants on everything
we loved this suggested seriousness.
we were not allowed to love in any fickle way.

in the revisionist history of my hood genesis
i would be more honest than honest:
put things *on my huffy bike*
on my report card
on my citizenship award
on my mama's golden N.A. necklace
on my grandma's favorite chair
on my father's attention
& the warm air
he left
each time he fled.

after Pierre got shot & his bullet
gifter walked the same blocks
as the rest of us in uneasy omerta
i didn't think he died.
how could he when his name
became a vow for us all? each street

dispute punctuated with *On P* to prove
us tellers of truths.

when Bird got jumped,
his spinal column crushed,
i assume he made his street name
true. a different kind of flight.
everything sacred between Ragtown boys
now enveloped in the parchment
of *On Bird* & carried away.

conceal

grandma who kept books for a living
& read corner store romance novels

grandma who kept dictionaries on the kitchen table
& slurred words into contraction

grandma who taught me how to pass a poll test
& how to beat a draft exam

grandma who told me to study hard
& leave school if the NBA was an option

grandma who bought Black
& called us her little niggas with a smirk

grandma who taught me how to shoot a bank shot
& told me to quit the team if i rode bench

grandma who paid for cars in cash
& gambled herself broke on weekends

grandma who hid toy
guns i got as gifts

                & when
             she passed
              i pulled
          a real shotgun
           from the wall
           of her closet.

poem for Blacky

your name so given
after you called me Blacky
in Bart's basement
& i slid a hard cue ball
into your surprised white finger.

i ask about you more
than i do any of the other neighborhood
kids, the ones who were nice to me
or at least silent.
i consider you more now
than any of the girls down the block
with their quick smiles & snapping necks,
their fretful mothers peeking in the windows

my man Blacky
if we shook hands today
would your ring finger crook?

Blacky, we ate kielbasa
together & then beefed.

Blacky Blacky Blacky.
you, apology paid in pain.
little reversal of racism.
small justice of wrath.
my middle school jubilee.
my first tiny reparation.

my mother's hands

would moisturize
my face from jaw inward
the days she had too
much on her hands
when what needed
to come through
did or didn't show.
she still shone, still made
smooth her every rough
edge, heel to brow.
hugged my temples
with slick hands,
as if to say *son be mine*
as if to say *this i give you*
as if to say *we are people*
color of good oak but we
will not burn, we survive
every fire without becoming
ash.

after we stopped rap

a few are dead.

a bunch have moved away.

1 i heard works contracts
for the league's best.
another keeps bars in the gentry's
Brooklyn playground.
1 of the meanest i ever knew in a battle
is in L.A. scraping up for a headshot.
the rawest beatbox of all
is a stay-at-home dad in a suburb
so far from the fucked-up art galleries
where our shows were thrown
& sometimes packed & more often empty
except for us & the percussion.

the ones here are thrown
to the wind like dandelion fur.

a postal worker.
a teacher's assistant.
a grease-stained mechanic.

1 i know wants to break
into tech, thumbs coding books
like brittle vinyl.

a bunch of us work
with kids.
some are strung out.
at least 1 is getting a doctorate.
many of us sit on either side of a bar
at inappropriate hours.
some are locked down
or doing dirt that could get that done.

but i'm sure in the quiet hours
wherever we rest our heads
& hear a passing car
with the familiar thump
of a beat through too-thin apartment walls
or the bleeding bleat of a chorus
of crickets with a slick tempo
we nod.
we remain
heads.
we tip our temples
to this morse code.

welcome to how the hell i talk

population: all the *motherfuckers* i started
saying in front of my mother once i got to 18
alive & kidless & free.

climate: cold as in hot as in
i swear i'm cold on the mic not cold in
this game from the free throw line.

culture & contemporary life:
dear reader if i call you joe
know its synonym for cousin
or countryman. if i call you OG
it means mother or murder.

demographics: 35 percent Missibamaisiana-isms from the Up
    South old folks. 20 percent
magnet school doublespeak. 15 percent white girl whispering in
    the suburbs or summer camps.
18 percent too many rap records. 12 percent my mom's work voice.

economics: free lunch tickets & 75 cents
for the ice cream truck & FAFSA &
buying Link cards from someone's relative
for this month's groceries.

government: 2 branches
today. who knows what grows
tomorrow if i need to make magic

of my mouth for some hostile stranger
to see my human.

crime: dope cuz what my folks smoked,
sometimes sold. cuz the hip-hop songs
i sung until they got in my body like dope.

sister cities: my students in Cape Town who asked
what my mother tongue was since they didn't know no
Black folk with only English 1st. this the answer
i should've given.

geography: everything in my throat
i say & mean & shouldn't. how i
cuss like the big niggas in the neighborhood
cuz i was afraid to talk
in front of them. the gang lit
i know & should & shouldn't.
the truths i tell that i wish were game.
the verbal flourish that drops off like a waterfall.

what can be said

tonight, i'm feeling tender
because it's another time
with my granddaddy
& he's still here
& if he could remember i
would ask him about when he was young
what he would say to the women so they knew
he meant whatever he wanted them to know he meant.
but he's not here in that way so i say
how you living young man
& he answers *slow motion*.
     (& i believe him because i can see him tentative
     when he lifts himself out of the chair.)
once Alzheimer's does what it do
you never really have conversations
it's more a man becomes a poem
a lot of repetition & love with something
indecipherable in between.

African american literature

i like your poems because they seem so real.
i like your poems because they seem so real.
i like your poems because they seem so real.
i like your poems because they seem so real.

i like your poems because they seem so real.
i like your poems because they seem so real.
i like your poems because they seem so real.
i like your poems because they seem so real.

i like your poems because they seem so real.
i like your poems because they seem so real.
i like your poems because they seem so real.
i like your poems because they seem so real.

i like your poems because they seem so real.
f'sho, good look, this also a sonnet.

FINNA is not a word

Hope is a discipline.
—MARIAME KABA

my word of the day is: ideation.
this is definitely a word, certainly
in any good dictionary. ideation as in
██████ ideation. a few days ago
my word of the day came up as renege.
sometime before that it was sawbuck,
before that; woo woo this.
sometimes, i believe in all that my people make their mouths do.
other days, i read books on grammar & proper style, correct
my own usages.
in those times my language is elevated,
my diction is deliberate.
my mind, undisciplined
& spinning.

I THOUGHT THIS POEM WAS FUNNY
BUT THEN EVERYBODY GOT SAD

your mama so Black
her neighborhood is
half bandos & blue lights.

wait lemme try again.

    knock knock.
          who there?
the debt collector.

    no knock.
          who there?
police.

so a guy walks into a bar
      & gets carried out.
so a woman walks into a bar
      & gets carried out.
so i don't believe in gender
      but payroll does.

& what's the deal with sweaters
& what's the deal with sweatshops
& what's the deal with this shop
i copped this sweater there
it was a deal.

what has a Black body
& is red all over?

        i mean is read all over

           i mean

                that's the punch line.

inner child age projection: 57 years old

working out is the province of a depressive, every day
discovering another *not anymore,* the body's small
failures compiling where competence was. the old
nigga hooping has the vantage of knowing he is his
shadow. he learns angles & patience, how to see
where the ball will be. he knows to jump without leaving
ground. he sees younger models gazelle foolish across
the court & hears where to interrupt their dribble rhythm.
the game he plays is wisdom. he feels how to not bend
at the knees, such fickle joints. his hips, thick with slow
metabolism, do the work of nudging space enough.
nigga no longer athletic but effective enough to not
lose. the first woman he loved is another man's forever.
his homies are dead or married. possibly imaginary.
every time he shaves his head it is quicker work,
a job disappearing, another cartilage weakening.
each time his vocal cords wear & fail the power
stays out longer, the jaw muscles too weak to force
an audible syllable.

dispatch from the 6th circle

CRAWFORDSVILLE, IN

i count the Confederate flags
around town, a surprise considering the geography.
what earnest confusion, honest mistake it takes
to fly a rebel flag in the North. this makes the most
sense: us turning against us, the cannibal instinct, the
vote against self. self-hate is something i've known.
hear the way my voice lilts too many
ways, my vocabularies wrestle themselves, scrap
amongst the street in between my teeth. watch my mouth slang
& stutter into eloquence. watch my mouth whistle
this simple Dixie.

publicist

a mentor told me
to consider writing
essays that commemorate
days that relate to my book.
it's a good way to insert
your work into the public
conversation. well motherfuckers
spend every day killing
a Black somebody in Chicago
& every next day the whole world
practices saying silences like
Black on Black
gang related
violent neighborhood
so i guess i owe a
million essays.
i guess my book
will be huge.

when america writes

about Black life
they prefer the past

                                                    tense.

Oregon Trail

for my great aunt & Jonathan Hicks

my first venture west was in Windows 98
or Independence, Missouri. class was in the computer lab
& we were supposed to be playing some typing game.
the one i remember had a haunted theme.
ghosts instructing us on the finer points of where
to put our fingers. these were the last days
before keyboards as appendage, when typing
was not nature. i should've been letting an apparition
coach me through QWERTY but rather
i was at the general store deciding between ammo & axles,
considering the merits of being a banker or carpenter.

too young to know what profession
would get me to the Willamette Valley
in the space of a 40-minute period.
i aimed my rifle with the arrow keys, tapped the space
bar with a prayer for meat to haul back to the wagon.

this game came difficult as breathing underwater after
trying to ford a river.

i was no good at survival.
somebody always fell ill or out into the river.
each new day scurvy or a raid was the fate of a character
named for my crush or my baby sister.
this loss i know, how to measure what it means
to die premature before a school period ends.

i can't understand the game coming to a late end.
an elderly daughter grieving her elderly mother.
reading the expansive obit in a suburban
Detroit church is a confusing newness.

when the old do the thing the world expects
i retreat into my former self. focus on beating
video games I've always sucked at, brush up
on Chicago Bulls history, re-memorize
the Backstreet Boys catalog, push
away whatever woman is foolhardy enough
to be on any road with me. i pioneer my way away
from all the known world. i look at homicide rates
& wish we all expired the way i know best. i pray
for a senseless, poetic departure. i pray for my family
to not be around to miss me while i'm still here.
i want a short obituary, a life brief & unfulfilled,
the introductory melody before a beat's crescendo into song,
the game over somewhere in the Great Plains.

i want to spare my descendants the confusion
of watching a flame flicker slow. keep them from being
at a funeral thumbing the faded family pictures like worn keys,
observing the journey done, the game won, the west
conquered.

wednesday feels like a funeral

November 9, 2016

> or rather
a wednesday
in a body
such as mine.

what i know
of hate
i learned early
& then every
day after that.

this is my niece's
home. this is where
my nephew plays
until he don't play.

this is where my grandmothers
smoked themselves into graves &
my grandfathers lost their heads
in many ways.

what place i know
other than this hate crime with
geography attached. i don't
speak nothing but this. my only
tongue is this broken-winged pidgin.

my only song is this crooked
anthem. *Oh say*
i don't remember
& i can't forget.

let me put it to you like this fam

terrorists are thugs are freedom
fighters are police are gang
members are cousins are politicians
are teachers are protectors are
love are loathing
depending on your vantage point.

like the time them guys jumped me & tried to run
my pockets they were frantic & afraid & i
could tell because of the shallow, quick kicks
they offered to my skinny body.

i think they meant to rob me but they ran
their hands into the wrong pocket first cuz i'm left
handed so in a sense writing didn't save my life but it kept
my few few dollars & my bus card from disappearing.
O, writing the savior of my state
ID.

these dudes were about the same
size as me but they were 4 & i a single
me & when they got off the bus at my stop i noticed
they wore all the name brands we loved but can't remember now.
my gear was anonymous & dark like our Black faces. i was
just a hoodie & a surprising punch back.

these days i think about how they slipped
my knees from behind & had all the leverage
to stomp whatever part of me & didn't. bless them.

praise that day i became
a polytheist. praise my 4 gods & i pray
for my 4 gods as often as i pray
for myself. praise the gods they find
or will find or who have found them
in churches & parties & coffins
& corner stores.

i'm saying this, cats could really end
a mog if they had better aim or worse aim,
depending on your vantage point. it's like bad
meaning bad or bad meaning good.
i mean it's like not believing in police
because you don't believe police
when they sit in your mama's house & tell her nothing
can be done cuz they don't do things really.

it's like believing in gangs
because the pass they gave you,
the strong dap & safe haven
to go on being bookish
& breathing & walking in the hood.

let me put it to you like this fam:
who you believe in is a matter
of who you mattered to.

FINNA

every line i write shrieks there are no easy solutions.

—AUDRE LORDE

what it is & will be

ain't yet no word for a world without the cop's unruly bullet or baton.

ain't yet no word for a world without children starved & lonesome.

ain't yet no word for a world with boundless capacity for care.

ain't yet no word for a world with every bloody debt repaired & repaid.

ain't yet no word for a world with touch exclusively consensual & ecstatic.

ain't yet no word for a world where each mistake is a holy possibility to improve.

ain't yet no word for a world where there are as many genders as dandelion seeds spinning in Spring.

ain't yet no word for a world where every person is vegan & the last meat they ate was the rich.

ain't yet no word for a world with no fear.

ain't yet

but we working.

aubade for the whole hood

today i offer my self
all the small kindnesses.

i'm out here
with breath in my body
though it may be stank
& body in my control
though it may be too much
or not enough.

today i offer the whole crib
a jam we ain't heard in a minute
& permission to turn the news down
& move a hip like a suggestion
to a lover.

on this day i declare the pockmarked
street i grew up on a miracle.
i declare the bills, even the overdue
ones, a blessing. who knew
that we would still be here
to see these injustices. how can we measure
the disrespect of lack against that precious surprise?

real talk,
today i tell myself truths
other than the one that makes me low,
i give myself the gift of a joke with the homies.

real talk,
today i stay woke
to all the terror
but also to my favorite food
or my favorite place
or my best hope for our people
& i work to make all
my best lives possible.

another Nate Marshall origin story

pardon my French
but all i do is make meaning
out of some ole bullshit
bae boy you ain't making
nothing i'm not up on.
all i do is curse by using
my own language
all my language profane
all my slang is a vial from
God's vein.
all my words cursive
all my name is my name
taken. call me D'Nealian,
begat by Palmer begat by James
begat by James Sr. begat by some
brother in the wind i don't know.
all my names made
by men. all my names man made
all my names made up.
all my names makeup.
all my names make men.
all my names are mine
even if they made up
even if i made them up.
all my names a poem.
all my names a song.
all my names do is sing.
all mine.

hecky naw

before hell was an address we knew to call
we were only allowed to utter hecky naw.

the extra y, as if a question hanging in air—
can we get some more mom? hecky naw.

at the courts, we were picked up or picked on.
can i run in the next game? negro hecky naw.

when Kanye was cartographer of our grammar—
1st album, he told us *aw hecky naw*

that boy is raw. & of course, we all wanted
to be so uncooked, so rare. were we? hecky naw,

just a bunch of grayed knees & hard heads,
nate & his boys playing manhood. convincing? hecky naw.

imagine

you better imagine
like your life depends
because it does.

that boredom out of which making
is made is the only thing.

consider that somebody first had to pick through all the prehistoric
    plants
& sniff & taste
& sometimes diarrhea or even die
just so you would know that a collard green with the right seasoning
is a season that lasts centuries.

consider that somebody gazed at a star & said
aight bet
& built a fire.

consider the first Negro
on the first plantation
who figured which way was north
maybe before they knew the word
for north
& ran.

consider my love
with the middle name the enslaved dreamed of
running towards. see how i move swift in her direction.
consider how love is a great idea
we keep having every day. we imagine
being together & that is the first step.

which art? what fact?

everyday i act permanent: a silly collection of carbon
& oxygen & sometimes heart & too often cruelty
or callous or *i just wasn't thinking, my bad.*
each week i move around
as if nobody will steal me
again, or my things again.
& i ponder if which museum
we end up in is a matter of power,
who hangs & who does the cutting.

after all what is science
but a set of contemporary creation stories
what histories are natural & what artifacts art?
how do we decide the borders of a country
or an era or a solar system? when did we decide
our planet meant only this collection of green?

what i mean is this: take this bowl
the people used to mix & eat.
what of the clothes the people wore
to say *let us be one*
on this day of marriage? what of this
staff the people made to love
their gods? what of their gods
who are maybe our own with the names that lost,
the prayers that got colonized away?

in the section of the museum for the darker people
i make sense. in the museum of Chicago i have always been
in the section for the darker people
& i presume once this president or the next wipes us up
perhaps our everyday particulars will be art.
the afro pick i push in the naps of my beard
might one day have a name & a plastic box for preservation.
maybe the cheap dress shoes i spun in for my first
high school homecoming will be a prime example of primitive garb
for worship. maybe my mother's coffee cup with lipstick
kissed on its chipped face will be one of these art things in its next life.

O whatever God or whatever ancestor that wins in the next life
i pray let me be an artifact of use. let all my poems be
bowls or thrones or hairpieces or marriages.
let everything i make, if it should survive, tell the next world
mine were a people of faculty & faith. let them know
we were a race who prayed with our legs & sweat.
let them know that even when we are just art
we were here
& we still are.

fiddy'leven

how much is owed
to those who wore
the chains who tilled
the land who nursed
the babes who mixed
the grits who fried
the food who chopped
the wood who picked
the bolls who ran
the road who fought
the war who shared
the crop who made
the name who wore
the noose who Blacked
the codes who sparked
the schools who juked
the blues who showed
the soul who left
the south who stayed
the course who caught
the hell who marched
the march who broke
the strike who struck
the blow who took
the vote who held
the hood who housed
the club who queered
the notes who spun
the jams who funked

the flow who built
the thing who built
the thing who built
the thing? you know.

take the payment
you ain't give
for all that & press
it down, make it
overflow fiddy'leven
times & gimme that.
in my own numbers
of my own currency.

FINNA

for Juanita & the Perspectives Leadership Academy Class of 2016

so this one time i was finna say finna in a academic context
& a voice in my head said *shouldn't you be worried*
about using a word that ain't a word & i was like *word.*

& for a long time that was how i let my life happen,
i let my mind tell me a million nos that the world
had implanted in me before i even formed questions.
i let my power be dulled by my fear of fitting.

but i remember a million finnas
i avoided to get here. like the day
them dudes jumped me off the bus & i was finna
get stomped out like a loose square. or the day
they got to shooting at the park & i was finna
catch one like an alley-oop. or the day
my grandma died & my grades dropped & i was finna
not finish high school except i had a praying mama
& good teachers & poems to write. i'm thankful for all these finnas
that never were & when i remind myself
of who i've always been i remember why
my finna is so necessary.

finna comes from the southern phrase *fixing to*
like i come from my southern grandmothers & finna
is this word that reminds me about everything next.
even when i've been a broken boy i know i'm fixing to
get fixed. i'm finna be better. every dream i have is a finna

away from achievement. each new love i uncover is a finna
i unfold. every challenge i choose to meet & not let defeat me is a finna
i fight for.

my hope is like my language is like my people: it's Black
& it's brown & it's alive
& it's laughing & it's growing & it's alive
& it's learning & it's alive & it's fighting & it's alive
& it's finna
take on this wide world
with a whole slang for possibility.

&nem

&you too if you feel it.
&you know by feel it
i don't mean bought it
&i don't mean studied.
&you know by feel it
i mean
the whole nation head nodding
to niggas they tried to lock up or out
or i mean my whole talk a cakewalk
every time i'm on the phone tricking you
into my humanity or on my CV deceiving
you into hiring a maroon.

&you know by feel it
i don't mean
you opted in. i mean my people here
&been here making genius from gristle
&every moment you declare a renaissance
is just every moment you fools been paying
the right attention.
&we not stuttin that cuz we'd rather you pay
reparations.

&attention my good people
or bad people
or not people:
what you do unto the least you do unto me.
cuz every time you decided i was acceptable

or articulate or actually okay
you don't know who you let in.

you let in my mama
&my daddy
&my greasy greasy grandmammy
&my hood
&my woes
&all the folks who taught my flows
&my thugs
&my killers
&all the ones you think are drug dealers
&my people
&my people
&my people
&my people
&my fine fine fine
people
&nem.

Acknowledgments

Damn we did it. I have a lot of love for a lot of people who helped make this book happen & I'm sure I will forget some, but I want to name a few who have been invaluable.

My love, Alison C. Rollins.

My family: Mama & Daddy & Meecie & Kay-Kay & Tasha & Nita & Jus & Granddaddy & my aunties & uncles & cousins & nem.

My crew, Dark Noise (Fatimah Asghar, Franny Choi, Aaron Samuels, Danez Smith & Jamila Woods).

Mi hermano, José Olivarez.

The whole One World team, especially my incredible editor, Nicole Counts.

The whole BEOTIS team, especially my genius agent, Tabia Yapp.

The wide net of homies who've helped catch & keep me while

writing this book: Kaveh Akbar, Hanif Abdurraqib, Eloisa Amezcua, P. Scott Cunningham, Zain Aslam, Kasey Anderson, Clint Smith, Cortney Lamar Charleston, Camonghne Felix, Eve L. Ewing, Ydalmi Noriega, Diamond Sharp, Adam Levin, Ben Spacapan, Casey Hicks, Shaun Peace, Lamar Appiagyei-Smith, Araba Appiagyei-Smith, Erika Stallings, Jeremy McCarter, Charlene Carruthers, Bryson Whitney, Christian Nuñez, Jeremy L. Williams, Chris Marve, Morgan Parker, Katy Richey, Immanuel Mitchell-Sodipe, Britteney Black Rose Kapri, Kevin Coval, Jalen Kobayashi, Sabrina Thomas, Michael Sawyer, Peter Kahn, Tess Raser, H. Melt, Angel Nafis, Paul Tran, Safia Elhillo, Chris Nuñez & anybody else I forgot charge it to my head not my heart.

Thanks to all the journals and publications that let these joints stretch they legs and get to fighting weight: *The Offing, Kenyon Review Online, Split Lip Magazine, The Adroit Journal, The Shallow Ends, BOAAT Journal, The Fight & The Fiddle, The Rumpus, The End of Chiraq, Columbia Poetry Review,* Academy of American Poets Poem-a-Day, *Chicago & Poetry.*

Thanks to the institutions who've supported this work, including Colorado College, Wabash College, the Poetry Foundation, Young Chicago Authors & Cave Canem.

Thank you to the city. Chicago over Everything. South Side over that. Wild Hundreds over all.

NATE MARSHALL is an award-winning author, editor, poet, playwright, performer, educator, speaker, and rapper. His book *Wild Hundreds* was honored with the Black Caucus of the American Library Association Literary Award for Best Poetry and the Great Lakes Colleges Association New Writers Award. He is also an editor of *The BreakBeat Poets: New American Poetry in the Age of Hip-Hop*. Marshall is a member of the Dark Noise Collective and co-directs Crescendo Literary with Eve L. Ewing. He is an assistant professor of English at Colorado College. Nate was born and raised on the South Side of Chicago. He holds an MFA in creative writing from the University of Michigan's Helen Zell Writers' Program and a BA in English and African American Diaspora Studies from Vanderbilt University. Marshall has received fellowships from Cave Canem, the Poetry Foundation, and the University of Michigan.

nate-marshall.com
Twitter: @illuminatemics
Instagram: @illuminatemics